MAJOR SPORTS EVENTS

THE SUPER BOWL

BY BO MITCHELL

WWW.APEXEDITIONS.COM

Copyright © 2023 by Apex Editions, Mendota Heights, MN 55120. All rights reserved. No part of this book may be reproduced or utilized in any form or by any means without written permission from the publisher.

Apex is distributed by North Star Editions:
sales@northstareditions.com | 888-417-0195

Produced for Apex by Red Line Editorial.

Photographs ©: Lynne Sladky/AP Images, cover; Mark LoMoglio/AP Images, 1, 27; Ben Liebenberg/AP Images, 4–5, 29; Mark J. Terrill/AP Images, 6, 8–9; National Photo Company Collection/Library of Congress, 10–11; Tony Tomsic/AP Images, 13, 22–23; Shutterstock Images, 14, 15, 16–17, 18–19, 20–21, 21; AP Images, 24–25

Library of Congress Control Number: 2022912148

ISBN
978-1-63738-295-0 (hardcover)
978-1-63738-331-5 (paperback)
978-1-63738-401-5 (ebook pdf)
978-1-63738-367-4 (hosted ebook)

Printed in the United States of America
Mankato, MN
012023

NOTE TO PARENTS AND EDUCATORS

Apex books are designed to build literacy skills in striving readers. Exciting, high-interest content attracts and holds readers' attention. The text is carefully leveled to allow students to achieve success quickly. Additional features, such as bolded glossary words for difficult terms, help build comprehension.

CHAPTER 1
SUPER BOWL CHAMPIONS 4

CHAPTER 2
SUPER BOWL HISTORY 10

CHAPTER 3
REACHING THE SUPER BOWL 16

CHAPTER 4
SUPER MOMENTS 22

COMPREHENSION QUESTIONS • 28
GLOSSARY • 30
TO LEARN MORE • 31
ABOUT THE AUTHOR • 31
INDEX • 32

CHAPTER 1

Super Bowl Champions

Less than two minutes are left in the Super Bowl. The Los Angeles Rams are facing the Cincinnati Bengals. The Bengals are up by four points.

The Rams played the Bengals in Super Bowl LVI. The game took place on February 13, 2022.

The Rams' quarterback makes a pass. The receiver catches the ball in the **end zone**. It's a touchdown! Los Angeles takes the lead.

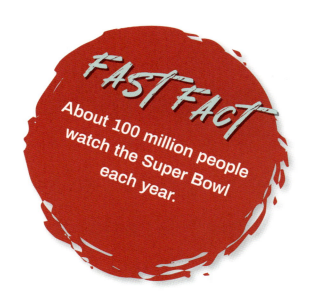

FAST FACT
About 100 million people watch the Super Bowl each year.

Rams quarterback Matthew Stafford (9) passes for a touchdown near the end of Super Bowl LVI.

The Rams hold on to the lead. They become National Football **League** (NFL) **champions**. Players raise the trophy to celebrate.

Rams players celebrate with the Lombardi Trophy after winning Super Bowl LVI.

THE LOMBARDI TROPHY

The Lombardi Trophy goes to the Super Bowl winners. It's named after Vince Lombardi. He coached the Green Bay Packers. He helped them win the first two Super Bowls.

CHAPTER 2

SUPER BOWL HISTORY

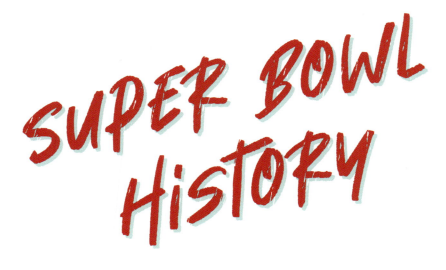

Professional football began in the 1890s. In 1920, the NFL formed. The American Football League (AFL) started in 1960.

Players compete in a football game during the 1920s.

At first, the two leagues were totally separate. That changed in January 1967. The best NFL team played the best AFL team. This game became known as the Super Bowl.

FAST FACT

In 1970, the AFL joined with the NFL. They formed one league.

Bart Starr helped Green Bay defeat Kansas City in the first Super Bowl.

Famous artists do a halftime show at the Super Bowl. The Weeknd played at Super Bowl LV.

The Super Bowl has taken place every year since. It quickly became one of the biggest sports events in the world.

CREATING THE NAME

The first Super Bowls had a different name. "Super Bowl" wasn't used until the third game. One team's owner came up with the name. His kids had a toy called a Super Ball.

The Super Bowl is known for its TV commercials. Companies pay lots of money to get ads during the game.

CHAPTER 3

REACHING THE SUPER BOWL

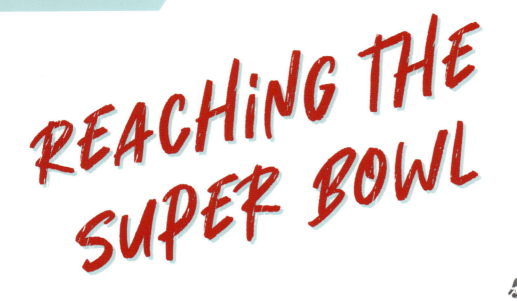

The NFL is made up of two **conferences**. One is the American Football Conference (AFC). The other is the National Football Conference (NFC).

As of 2022, each NFL conference had 16 teams. The Jets were in the AFC. The Falcons were in the NFC.

Teams play one another during the season. The best teams from the AFC and NFC make the **playoffs**.

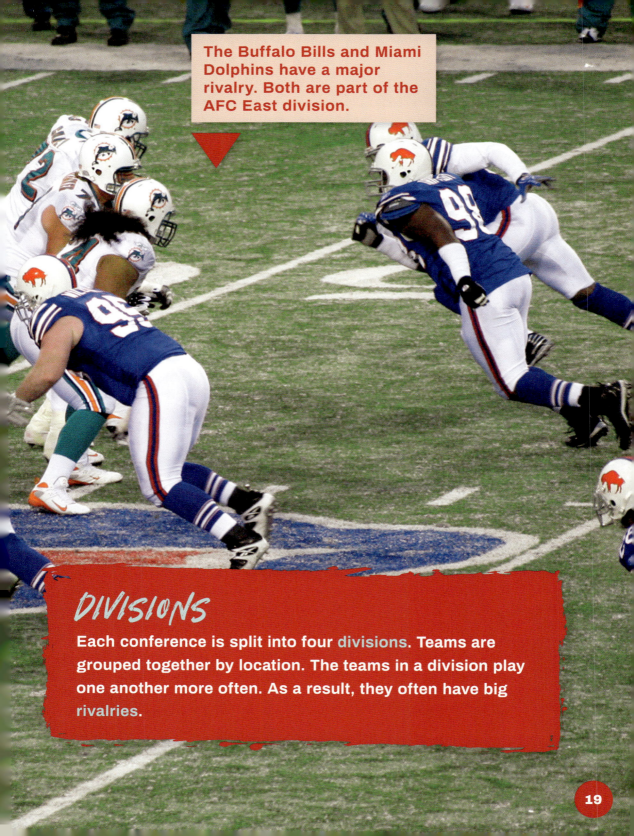

The Buffalo Bills and Miami Dolphins have a major rivalry. Both are part of the AFC East division.

DIVISIONS

Each conference is split into four divisions. Teams are grouped together by location. The teams in a division play one another more often. As a result, they often have big rivalries.

The playoffs are a **tournament**. Teams that lose are knocked out. Winning teams move on. The champions from each conference meet in the Super Bowl.

FAST FACT

After the big game, the winners get Super Bowl rings. These valuable rings are covered in diamonds.

The Super Bowl is held at a different stadium each year.

Super Bowl rings sometimes have team logos on them.

CHAPTER 4

SUPER MOMENTS

Experts thought the Baltimore Colts would win Super Bowl III. But Jets quarterback Joe Namath said his team would win. He was right. The New York Jets won 16–7.

Jets quarterback Joe Namath looks to pass during Super Bowl III in January 1969.

Miami's Jim Mandich makes a diving catch during Super Bowl VII.

In 1972, the Miami Dolphins won every game. They won Super Bowl VII, too. As of 2022, no other Super Bowl winner had ever finished undefeated.

FAST FACT
Super Bowls are numbered with Roman numerals.

Tom Brady won six Super Bowls with the Patriots. Then he helped the Tampa Bay Buccaneers win Super Bowl LV. He had more Super Bowl wins than any other player.

THE MOST SUPER BOWLS

As of 2022, no team had won more than six Super Bowls. Only two teams had won six. They were the New England Patriots and the Pittsburgh Steelers.

Tom Brady celebrates after the Buccaneers win Super Bowl LV.

COMPREHENSION QUESTIONS

Write your answers on a separate piece of paper.

1. Write a paragraph that explains the main idea of Chapter 3.

2. Do you usually watch the Super Bowl? Why or why not?

3. Which team won the first Super Bowl?

    A. Green Bay Packers
    B. Baltimore Colts
    C. Miami Dolphins

4. Which player had won the Super Bowl seven times as of 2022?

    A. Vince Lombardi
    B. Tom Brady
    C. Joe Namath

5. What does **valuable** mean in this book?

After the big game, the winners get Super Bowl rings. These valuable rings are covered in diamonds.

    A. free
    B. very common
    C. worth a lot

6. What does **undefeated** mean in this book?

In 1972, the Miami Dolphins won every game. They won Super Bowl VII, too. As of 2022, no other Super Bowl winner had ever finished undefeated.

    A. with only one win
    B. by winning the championship
    C. without losing a game

Answer key on page 32.

GLOSSARY

champions
Teams that win the final game in a conference or league.

conferences
Smaller groups of teams within a sports league.

divisions
Groups of teams within a conference.

end zone
The end of a football field where teams score touchdowns.

league
A group of teams that play one another.

playoffs
A set of games played after the regular season to decide which team will be the champion.

professional
Having to do with people who get paid for what they do.

rivalries
Sets of players or teams that really want to beat one another.

tournament
A competition that includes several teams.

BOOKS

Buckley, James, Jr. *Who Is Tom Brady?* New York: Penguin Workshop, 2021.

Morey, Allan. *The Super Bowl*. Minneapolis: Bellwether Media, 2019.

Scheff, Matt. *The Super Bowl: Football's Game of the Year*. Minneapolis: Lerner Publications, 2021.

ONLINE RESOURCES

Visit www.apexeditions.com to find links and resources related to this title.

ABOUT THE AUTHOR

Bo Mitchell has been writing about sports since the 1990s. He enjoys exercise, music, and hanging out with friends. Bo has lived in Minnesota his entire life. He hopes his favorite team, the Minnesota Vikings, will win the Super Bowl.

INDEX

A
American Football Conference (AFC), 16, 18
American Football League (AFL), 10, 12

B
Baltimore Colts, 22
Brady, Tom, 26

C
Cincinnati Bengals, 4

G
Green Bay Packers, 9

L
Lombardi Trophy, 9
Lombardi, Vince, 9
Los Angeles Rams, 4, 7–8

M
Miami Dolphins, 25

N
Namath, Joe, 22
National Football Conference (NFC), 16, 18
National Football League (NFL), 8, 10, 12, 16
New England Patriots, 26
New York Jets, 22

P
Pittsburgh Steelers, 26
playoffs, 18, 20

T
Tampa Bay Buccaneers, 26

ANSWER KEY:
1. Answers will vary; 2. Answers will vary; 3. A; 4. B; 5. C; 6. C